AF326714

APRIL SAVAGE

THE
WAY
IT
IS

SPLASH TIDE
—PUBLISHING—

Contents

Dedicated for survivors,

and in remembrance of those who didn't.

Keep going,

because the world needs you.

It will always need you.

The Table of Camaraderie

So, come sit with me at my table,

because I have food for you to eat

and plenty of things to drink,

to give you nourishment and hope,

to encourage your soul

And there will be laughter and fun,

for the love will never run cold

It doesn't matter if you are dying or thriving

Doesn't matter your scars or pain,

or choices that have driven you insane

Camaraderie doesn't judge your looks or illness,

and although your scars the world can see,

I, too, have scars that bleed deep

So, come and sit with me,

and let's eat

I:
ENOUGH

The Pussy

Surrender is not a strong vice

It's an abandon of free will

It's a painstaking effort to take what cannot be stilled

So, we fight to share a voice of reason,

met with opposition screaming,

halting truths of our dead-upon-arrival-ambitions

We bleed to death from wounds never healed

and if we survive,

the scars thrust upon us

are hated and judged as pride,

but we just want to have rights for our life

so, we'll die standing for what is right

We see the future and breathe oppression

refusing to writhe in the world's obsessions

As we fight for justice to protect those in need,

we'll not cower upon our knees

at the feet of a dirty old disease

Something so powerful is also beautiful in song,

but it's taken and pillaged

as if we have no rights at all

It's ours alone, so take your controlling fingers off

It's part of us as deep as our soul,

but the world judges how it lives and falls

It does not belong to the world, ever, at all,

and greed is the death of us all

It should not be kept in detriment,

but the depraved crawl to it like a slithering snake

desperate and needy,

like a prison of endless wanton,

laced with false treaties

It's a banshee screaming in the endless darkness

as death finds us

Society is wrong with its pleasure and pain

Society is broken due to its groping and gain

It's beautiful when held as a priceless treasure

in the arms of someone who'll truly

cherish it forever

True love protects

something so private and prolific,

admiring its delicate, yet powerful decisions

Wars prolong great pain

as battles stretch out when mercy flees,

and the actions of cruelty's demise

show the horrific pain since the dawn of time

Thievery is the most painful of all

because it takes something pure

to places it does not belong

Greed may throb erect and hard

and values thrust in and out all day long

Morality is dead as it exhausts itself til rising dawn,

turning under tangled sheets for more,

as death awaits to exploit it at the malicious doors

As humans birthed from our bodies

come with great pain and toil,

the wicked seeking to control it must also know:

to rule something that intricate

created to be so powerful,

shows the pussy rules the world

We've known it all along

so, fuck this never-ending song

Virtue

Virtue is not completely lost

when the valiant

stand and say:

No,

it will no longer be this way

The Penis

Society screams it's all about pleasure,

but true love craves a priceless treasure

to hold and cherish forever

We hunt with fervor

and desperate ambition,

to find the ones taken into sick derision

In the darkness,

morality is forsaken,

but we find you there,

at the doors of malicious intentions

We deliver the innocent

from the snakes and pigs,

so, the weak can finally live

Until then, we ready our swords

to strike down the greedy

Their twisted hands will be crushed and left needy

Our ambition will not fail

as we instill morality and reason

We fight battles of a never-ending war

to protect the ones who fall

Morality looks dead and weak,

but we are here to make the wicked bleed

We see your horrific pain and toil,

standing beside you to encourage

and watch you grow

It seems as if mercy has fled

as wars drag on and on,

but we keep our battle cries to continue on

So, fuck the wicked ones

and their twisted depravity

of a blood-drenched song

Valiant

The valiant

do not give up

we hear the screams,

we fight for the weak,

so, we can all breathe

Pick One

If we must have

one way or the other,

if we cannot choose

our own sisters and brothers,

and forced to watch

the rot from others,

but are told to pick one

over the other

as if the high and mighty

are the end decision,

then pick a finger

and watch it grow,

because my people

are no longer willing to sacrifice

for these inhumane tolls

The Audacity

I won't be silent, she said

knowing it could cost her everything

The audacity! They screamed

I won't stay down, she bled,

tormented by the sting of their blades

The audacity! They wailed

I will fight for the weak and needy, she breathed

So, the oppressors came,

accusing her of having the audacity

of giving, and living, and breathing hope

for those who cannot help themselves

Is the audacity bold in a time of need?

Or is the audacity the impudence of endless greed?

The Trees of Us

You're stubborn, they say.

You never listen or sway.

You do not walk with them or crave the line.

You buck at societal norms and roll your eyes.

And when they demand you step in line,

you turn the other way,

creating your own path.

If it's through briar patches or endless thorns,

even when you are slashed open and torn,

you are willing to walk the world all on your own,

because trees always find a way to grow.

Just Leave Him

Just leave him, they say,

but I have nowhere to live

without what he pays.

Just leave him, they say,

but our children will suffer

in worse, inhumane ways.

Just leave him, they say,

but my job does not pay a living wage.

Just leave him, they say,

but then I will be a burden,

that's what they'll say.

I guess I will just go live under a bridge,

and have my children taken away,

because I am a vessel unworthy

of what men get paid.

Just leave him makes no sense

unless the ones screaming it

can deliver her from the abyss.

Unless the ones telling her

can also lift her to be able to make a living

for her and the kids.

Unless the law steps in

and protects them from him.

Unless the judges ensure

she has rights, even though

she has nothing because of him.

Unless she is empowered

to survive and win.

Unless she believes her worth

after years of being torn down,

over and over again.

Just leave him, they say,

while judging her for the decisions she

has been forced to make

that cost her everything.

When Hope Wins

The child does not go hungry

and continues to learn

The mother does not get left behind

just because she stayed home with a child

and had to forfeit a career for a while

The man does not get judged

because of the color of his skin or accent

and the family gets to live

where they need opportunities to survive

When hope wins,

we all get fed

I Sat Where You Are,
Once

I see you there,

wallowing in the mud.

I feel your pain there,

as you squirm and roll in it.

But you can't scream for help

because your quivering mouth is full

of broken words that died inside you,

forsaken, forlorn, lonely and hated.

You've sown doubt

like streams of unending sorrow,

and you've bled yourself dry

as if famine is your mate.

And I stopped as I noticed you,

because every person walked by

as if you are the plague.

So, here is my hand, take it.

It's okay,

I sat where you are, once,

and now it's my turn,

because I remember the mud

that nearly took my life,

but what I remember the most

is the goodness of the one who

pulled me from my plight.

The Judge of Me

It is not the world or what it wants me to be

It is not my endless hardships

uncertainties, or enemy

It is my view of myself as it berates me

It is my own self-worth that screams:

She is not worthy

So, I must stand for myself,

and who I want to be,

because as my mind plays

the cruelest jokes upon me,

I know I will always be the worst

of the judge of me

Skeletons Can Grow

You knew and did nothing

You saw and said nothing

You pushed it under the rug,

like a naughty child

who was told to clean their room

But instead, the child pushed

the toys under the bed

where they thought no one could see

Yet here I am,

investigating the truths about me,

to heal and grow from the trauma you sowed

And all you have left are the

skeletons in your closet,

and now we all know that

skeletons can grow

It Never Matches

My strength doesn't need to match

your worldview,

or how you fail to see.

You weren't there to see

what it did to me.

My shoes don't need to walk

the paths you've taken,

or are currently on.

Turns out,

our styles were different all along.

Number

How can you say

you want the best for me,

and for me to be a part of this society

when you take away

my right to even breathe,

because you reduced me to a number?

A number unseen,

except for the profit it brings.

A number spewed out

in your never-ending greedy machine.

In fact, it's not about being human at all.

It's not about helping those who fall.

It's just a number demanding attention.

It's just a number screaming,

these are for my intentions.

It's a number dictating we step in line

or stay down,

and God forbid we

listen to morals instead of you clowns!

You say we need to be a part of society

but you reduced us to a number

in your grand scheme of greed.

I'm just a number, after all

and when I take my last breath,

I'll still be a number

even in death,

according to your oppressive laws.

I Will Buy it Anyway

So, you have piercings and art on your arms.

Maybe you have scars

from all the times you fell hard.

So, you have a different style

that makes you who you are.

I don't care.

I'm still going to smile and look you in the eyes.

I'm still going to order my coffee with pride.

And I'll come back,

and bring my friends, too.

I am different, too

and have no right to judge you.

Why the Child

Bugs are squashed for just existing,

even at times there is no rhyme or reason,

as mankind reserves the decision of what exists.

But why the child?

Flowers burst from soil and cling to the light,

as dew kisses them from morning to night.

They are plucked up and suffer slow deaths.

But why the child?

Trees are cut to make way for more greed,

to build towns or skyscrapers,

or whatever humans need,

and wildlife is left scrambling for homes

they once had in their short lives.

But why the child?

There is no greater hope than a child.

There is no hurtful demise in their eyes,

unless it is put there with malicious intent

to take, plunder and desecrate.

The future of our whole planet

rests upon the innocent born into it.

The dark hands of those hurting children

have no vision for the future of our existence.

But they must see their demise

and know humans do not live forever,

so, they take and plunder

in their declining hands of cruelty,

but really, they have a limited mentality,

and a twisted sense of morality.

But, why the child?

It will always and forever be

the weakest among us who suffer unjustly,

because the hands of greed do not know empathy.

But the world is getting older

and the ones harming them will, too.

Time often spews justice in ways we never knew.

As we rot in the earth bugs eat our remains,

and flowers grow as the dew covers our graves,

and the wildlife shits upon what remains.

My Shoulder is Yours

You may think people don't

see you when you fall,

or when your heart breaks,

but people like me do.

We see you, and feel you,

and have hopes for you, too.

Now, let me come closer

and put my arm around you.

You can cry on my shoulder,

for I know what it's like

to have no one to cry on, too.

Dirty

They are judged for being dirty,

but the dirtiest among us are the ones

who refuse to see past the disability,

or the pain of life's doubts.

They are ones who turn their backs

on those who cannot shout for help.

The dirty are the ones

who destroy lives with their power and clout.

They are the ones who could care less

of the needy who cannot move about,

or the ones who are desperate for relief.

As promises were made by those in power,

now it's nothing but endless grief.

The helpless are saddled with frustration

and know full well their desperation,

and judged for being a burden upon society.

It's up to the compassionate to bring them relief,

because the real dirty ones could care less

about helping those in need.

Greedy Pockets

We saw what you accepted,

laced with malice, bleeding with intentions.

You shifted your eyes from what mattered,

lining your pockets as if the streets are made of gold,

because of the lies you were told.

And the people you vowed to uphold

suffer as you sold them off,

because greed matters more

than the life you claimed you knew,

that put you in the position

to help those beneath you.

The Birds in my Head

The strict never took me,

and itineraries drove my insanity.

The schedule of mediocrity burdened me,

as I could never sit idle for long,

so, they called me impatient and ill-tempered.

They judged me as improper and unskilled,

but I was only being creative

with the hand life dealt me.

She'll never make it in real life, they said,

while trying to force me to change.

But the forcing opened a door within me

and birds flew out.

The oppression broadened my mind

until my wings sprouted out,

and then I could see what I was all about.

I would have known this about me,

if I had been encouraged all along,

but the world says no, do not let them follow

their own heart and do what they want.

Everyone is different in their own unique way.

Everyone has birds in their head

that sometimes come out to play.

People like me see the freedom early on,

even from far away,

and then dreams sprout something within us

that does not stay away.

It grows and festers until big ideas spew out,

and then the world wonders why

we don't fit in because we flounder in and out.

In a world that forces us to suppress

what we are really about,

the birds in my head are free to play.

Sometimes, cardinals transform into blue jays,

and that's okay.

I can be myself, even if I am all alone,

and though I may always be judged,

I am not wrong for being who I am.

So, let the birds come out.

You may be surprised at your creative side,

and shame on those who suppress

what you are really about.

Expectations

It's a led weight

like a looming mountain,

and I don't want to go places

making me combative.

It's a dry heave

laden with suffocation.

I don't want to drown

in its lies or obsessions.

Your expectations are not me,

or who I am meant to be,

even when society screams,

so, take your hands off of me.

The Lie of the Win

I came upon a priceless treasure

of beauty and peace.

It set my soul afire and put my mind at ease.

And I should have stopped there

to smile and ponder,

but instead, I scrolled some more

due to human wonder.

There were tons of content

shouting what it's all about.

You can do it! You belong!

But it only showed one side,

expecting everyone to follow along.

It did not acknowledge the broken ones

on the sidelines where life hits hardest of all.

The online world shows

who is the best and who is wrong.

It comes across as streams of empowerment,

but every single thing between the peace

were endless wins and tumultuous themes.

I wish we could forget these things,

but the haughty scream: More please!

So, I rolled my eyes and sighed inside.

I'm so damn tired of these endless rides.

I gazed out my window with weary eyes,

and realized I no longer cared

what anyone thought about my life.

The wins rule the world

with their glory and pride.

Then they gloat about gloating,

but it's an endless, dangerous ride.

It's okay to be proud of your win,

and help others who fall,

because encouragement delivers from

oppression when we need it most of all.

It's not the message dragging us down.

The lie of expectations makes everyone

try to be the same even when we don't fit in.

The world screams we don't belong,

but the world keeps dancing

around the same old songs.

I am Not

I am not a relic or a sad song

I do not bend or roll just to go along

I am not a lustful object of obsession

I can sense your fake intentions

I am not a piece of ass for your rage

for you to get off and then run away

I have no respect for your hate

or endless want

I am who I am and will not be bought

Power

You hide behind titles and prestige.

Your wealth is the source of all your sacred things.

And when you talk,

you don't talk to speak.

You spew nonsense to hurt people like me.

You talk to take the world's heartbeat,

and care more for your ambitions and greed,

as if every waking moment of your life

is not lived and breathed.

You are dead inside,

and rotted from the core.

We see what makes you breathe, but

do you even hurt or care, at all?

How dare I speak out or shout!

You may be in a position of power,

flaunting immorality with your greed,

but I would rather die on my feet

than get stranded on my knees.

So, the world bleeds,

and eventually,

we'll be rid of your unjust greed.

And then another one will come along,

to try to steal the worlds compassion song,

but it won't stop people like me

from speaking out against what's wrong.

Tell me Again

Tell me again

why flowers are encouraged to grow,

and spin and toil,

and fill the earth with beauty and color

in all their diverse shades of hope,

but we are not allowed

to grow, and spin and toil,

although we fill the earth with

beauty and color

and diverse shades of hope

Notification

Notifications make our society go round,

that's why we have endless pop-ups

to buy more stuff from then, here and now.

Subscribe to my newsletter to see what it's all about!

Hurry, before the sale is out!

Oh look, I'm doing this new thing, don't miss out!

I need more likes and clicks, so hear me out!

Oh damn, the filter failed, so now I am called out.

Go to this social media site, hurry, come on!

Download another app, but now it's time to get a new phone.

It's only been two years, after all.

What's another thousand dollars to continue

these harassments I cannot control all night long.

We cannot read an article or scroll in delight,

until something pops up like regurgitated slop.

And when we try to slide it to the side,

another window berates our time,

bragging about another endless ride.

And it'll come from a company

who doesn't care if you are sleeping,

dying, or struggling with life.

Unfollow. Block. Unfriend. Ah, such is life.

Accept these malicious cookies or you don't

get to see our site or move along.

I'd like to shove the cookies in places

darkness doesn't even belong.

Applying for a job?

Join our talent network to see if you belong!

Buy a suit to impress for an interview,

but once you're hired, people wear what they want.

We can still grab a book and dive inside,

and just let the words live in our minds,

and use our brains and creativity,

to see these worlds and how we think them to be.

Why is it people are reading less

if more decorations make books the best?

Pay us to get seen in the algorithm,

or die in the void among the others at sea.

But there's no guarantee!

I guess I will drown because my work is not worthy,

and money does not grow on trees.

Shit like this is why people hide from online society.

We do not play along, but online screams at us all day long,

that we must participate to be seen.

Is that all? No.

The CEOs are the ones winning, after all.

Oh shit, I clicked the link for the phishing bait,

and now it's too late!

Here's another class I have to take.

Let me check all these notifications

from people and groups

whom I do not know, nor do I belong.

What makes you think I want to join

the purple roosters gang page and song?

Ah, hell, why not? I should belong!

Oh, look, there's ten more groups just like it

to ride me til dawn.

Online screams the loudest by stringing us along.

Strangers we call friends are on

our personal pages for ages.

Let me weed you all out, since honestly,

I don't really know who any of you are.

But there are thousands of you, and

if you comment soon, you can stay on!

I crave attention, after all.

Let me publicly post another picture

of my underage child

for the world of strangers to gaze upon.

I'll be right back at it by dawn!

Driven

You're not stubborn, you're driven.

You're not broken, you're hurt.

You're not a hot mess,

you're busy, and life is not easy.

Not everyone knows you in and out.

Do not give up your dreams or ambition.

The world is not the one

living and driving your life.

Scars

I'm tired of hiding my scars

from pain and doubt.

I'm tired of covering up my heart

for a world that doesn't even let me shout.

I'm sick to death

of the endless lies of what life is about.

Just let me breathe and live

without these facades

taking me places I never wanted to go.

Just let me cry and moan,

even if the pain drives me low.

Sometimes we must get it out

before we blow.

How dare the world say:

you have no justification to feel this way,

when the world continues to cover up

the inside things that need to be said.

And even if scars never heal,

or never fade,

the world needs to see them,

because we are all only human.

If someone sees the pain,

they can step away with knowledge gained,

and share what they learned,

because there's always someone

hiding their scars from life,

and deep inside,

we all need to see a way to be

brought back to life.

Now Go

You can stomp on me

and stifle my hope

You can derail my thoughts

and cut my rope

But you don't get to tell me

how to live and go,

because although there are

floods, droughts, and endless storms,

flowers still find a way to grow

Linger

So, you thought you

could never breathe once broken?

That you could never change the world

because of all the lies you've been told.

You linger in and out, questioning your life,

as you struggle to fit the mold.

Darkness may saturate our lives

with endless pain and uncertain tolls,

but the light never dies, it lingers,

and light breaks the lies we are told.

Even the Air Is

You telling me it's not political

even as big companies

sow doubt, fear and pollution

in the water we drink,

and the air we breathe,

and the time we keep.

You telling me it's not political

when you guzzle natural resources

so, the machines can thrive,

but now we can't sleep at night,

or live our lives.

But hey, we have stolen art,

and people don't know how to write.

This is now humanities endless plight.

You telling me it's not political

when you took our rights

in the dead of night,

and we are too poor to fight.

But it is political,

when the very air we breathe

is sowed with discord and strife.

It is political,

when you take things from society

we need to live and thrive.

You keep taking our rights

and shortening our lives,

and then shout we are wrong

with your strong, unpolluted lungs

for breathing the air

and drinking the water

we all need to stay alive.

Motive

It's hard to see beyond the rubble of dreams,

or through the smoke of endless pain.

It's hard to breathe in this catastrophe,

as your motives breathe living flames.

And now I stand alone as a survivor,

with an orphaned cat clinging to me.

Its eyes are wide but dim,

and it shakes and moans

as blood pools from its limbs.

And I am too weak to pick it up,

because I am bleeding, too,

due to your motive of taking lives

from people you never knew.

Period

Gripe and moan about me being me

and what was given to me,

but I still need my rags for my bleed

I still need time to rest and relieve my pain,

because this body given to me

shows me no mercy

It aches and pains and bleeds

As it claws and rakes me inside,

the shallow men expect the best of me

to carry on and breed

They want the best of me

to look good and fulfill needs

And then when I am older,

and the world says, she is done,

look at what she has become,

when my body turns like a bloody sun

and rips me from the inside out

as if all I ever was

is a used vessel for pleasure, glory, and clout

then it's time to rip that organ out,

and the world says,

she is nothing now

but we can still bed her

and she can Botox the wrinkles out

I Gotta Know

Does it hurt you when I breathe?

When I climb the mountain peak?

Does it grate your nerves when I talk?

Especially when I speak up

for those with desperate needs?

How about when I step into the light,

and the darkness flees?

Or when I hold out my hand

to show the world how I bleed?

I gotta know how you see me

as you fake smile with malice in your eyes,

and the world needs to know, too,

because right now,

all I'm seeing from people like you

is hate for women like me

And you need to know

that I will continue to grow,

and talk about the ones who have needs

I will keep climbing so others know

the way to go,

and I will let the world see me bleed,

because I refuse to cover up

what your cruelty has done to me

Does it truly bother you to let me be me?

I gotta know, so the world can also see

The Round Table of Indecisions

I sat at a round table

to bring my life's worth

of the places I'd been,

the pain of the world,

and things about life that wore me thin

As I hoped to impart my wisdom,

I realized I did not fit in,

because they would not see past

the color of my skin, sex, or inhibitions

So, I stood and gazed to the clouds,

and turned back around and fled out

Then I walked the earth and gathered

ones around willing to listen

to what life is all about,

because although the table was round,

it was not whole

it was broken with greedy souls

Human

Is your blood and guts the source your life?

Does your heart ache when pain calls?

I have the right to be free and equal, after all.

For guts do not discriminate

and blood gives life for us all.

Are you free to walk about

without being taken or hauled off?

I have the right to be free from slavery and torture,

so, take your greedy hands of intent off.

I have the right to be recognized before the law.

Our insides scream equality remains

within our bones and veins,

and taking my right to justice tells me

you do not consider me human,

but a morsel to judge and to watch me fall.

Free me from your arbitrary detention, arrest or exile,

because I have the right to a fair trial.

Our insides tell a story,

presuming innocence until proven guilty.

Like when the doctor performs tests

to see diseases living within us

that may be our demise or unruly.

Even through this, I still have my privacy

and am free to move wherever I want,

and you've no right to take it just because you want.

When desperation comes,

I have asylum and can keep my nationality.

My genes were not created nor given by you,

and we are all different

in our pockets of the world.

I can own property, am free to marry and create a family,

and if I don't want to, it's not up to you.

I can have my own religion or beliefs,

for my insides don't care what expression I breathe,

in my freedom of assembly.

And if my expression doesn't match yours,

you still have no right to take mine

because I don't follow yours.

Public affairs are my right, as is social security,

and my right to work should also give me

rest and leisure time,

with an adequate standard of living.

I should not be a slave

to your corporate-driven capitalism.

I have the right to education,

to take part in cultural and scientific,

artistic life or endeavors.

So, give me more museums and libraries,

because knowledge is as powerful as empathy.

I have the right to a free and fair world,

and a duty to my community.

I've no right to judge my neighbor

for the color of their skin, accent or disability.

Yet history proves time and time again

that those oppressing basic human rights

will meet the cruelty of their repercussions,

while those denied basic rights are free to get justice.

Every human on the face of the planet

has a responsibility to respect

the human rights of others,

because we are all human.

Why do humans view so many others as lowly vessels?

Why do they see them as weak?

They stomp upon them and drive them to their knees.

They gnaw and gnash their jaws in jealousy or greed,

spewing hate about things

they do not know nor have ever seen.

And the oppression continues because

they are blind in their own hearts and minds,

yet we all have the same insides.

I am human.

You are human.

We are human.

We bleed the same.

Until we break down these cruel walls,

humanity will continue to fall.

This is not the world we want,

because human rights

belong to the whole world, after all.

II: THE PAIN THAT MADE ME

Humiliation

The weight of being so small

and made to feel so stupid

burdened me with an unloving pain,

but as I walked alone pondering my life,

a looming dark shadow blew over me,

so, I gazed up at its magnificent doom

as the cloud roared over me slowly,

and questioned why I had let the world

make me feel so small and stupid,

because the clouds are higher than us all,

and beyond the clouds, is the sun and moon

What I was Given

I was given an old, rusty bucket,

and the handle wobbled and creaked.

I was taught early on how to

fill and hold it, even though it leaked.

In time, I learned to rush

from the well to the basin

in my times of great need.

And there were many times I crawled

on my hands and knees, even as it leaked.

When the handle broke, it stabbed my knee,

and I turned to see

what my blood had given me.

I wobbled the worn path

I was told my whole life

were my hopes and dreams,

but it was what life had dealt me.

So, I climbed over the wall, bloody and weak,

desperate to live, finally.

I was given a choice of buckets,

and some were filled with hopes and dreams,

but many of them had nightmares,

and they screamed.

I chose one that was empty and new,

and I turned around and climbed

back over the wall with the knowledge that grew.

As I landed with grief,

my eyes beheld a lonely soul

who lay on their knees bleeding out.

So, I gave them the bucket of hope,

and nourished their wounds,

and pulled them up.

And then I turned to the well to help them all.

Sometimes, what we are given is not what we are.

Sometimes, what we find can be given

to help the ones who are held back,

so, they can finally climb over the wall.

Broken

I am not worthless

I'm judged

I am not helpless

I'm held back

I am not empty

I haven't been filled

I am not broken

I'm hurt

I am starving for food I cannot eat

I am desperate for hope I cannot see

I am craving freedom,

but not just for me

It doesn't matter the size of the boat

for hope sometimes comes

in small, uneven spurts

The waves roll over us all,

whether big or small,

because we all live in the sea

and it hurts the same, after all

Hell and Back

People who have been through hell

have a different light in their eyes

It's not dim, nor dying

It's a fire that breathes new life

When we see someone struggling,

we will take you off to the side,

put that fire in your eyes,

so, you can see a new life, too

The Voices

It's hard to see in the darkness

as it creaks and moans

We're left clawing at walls,

our fingers worn to the bone

We shift unsteady

as burdens drag us to our knees,

but we are desperate to see

If we close our eyes

and just breathe

something calls us out

The light isn't always seen

in our greatest times of pain

but hope makes us move about

because we have needs

The darkness cannot win

because the voices lift us up

and force you on your feet

and then you can carry on

So, carry on

because hope is not all gone

Bully

I came home from school upset and torn

the kids had judged me

and ridiculed me with scorn.

I was different from others and

would never be one of them.

I was like a round peg in a square hole

that would never fit in.

I sat on my bed,

my eyes full of tears.

My dad came in, and with sorrow in his eyes,

wrapped an arm around me with pride.

He encouraged me to stand for myself

and be brave and strong,

even when everyone judges me falsely

and thinks who I am is wrong.

As I grew, I remembered his voice.

So, when my own kids struggled,

I wanted them to also have a voice.

I taught them that endless bullshit

always comes because of a bully's cruel choice.

The weight of the world has always been

upon the shoulders of the strong all along.

Because the world is heavy and full of grief,

but people like us have the tools

to move forward and succeed.

Pain always haunts from time to time,

and it is not partial to the wealthy,

or those with no dimes.

You stand for yourself

and for others who cannot.

And now you know why the world

is full of gutless rot.

When the Light Hits

We sit at the table

when times are hard

and our hearts are

heavy with grief

and sometimes,

as the light shines in

we also see

the imprint of its hope

because it fades the tabletop

where we sat and moped

The Branch that Grew

I see your tree

and what you want to be,

but the soil is dry and lean,

so, here is my arm for you to cling,

and lean upon me

while you grow your dream

And if the soil holding you back

continues to stay lean,

you can uproot your tree

and cling to me,

and we will plant with purpose

the hope of your dreams,

and you can grow and thrive

in the right soil of your needs,

because we all need new trees

Living Scars

They breathe like fire

gnawing from the inside out

they never truly heal

and the world questions what they're all about

scars are judged as if they're

diseases to be wiped out

the world can scream all it wants

but life is hard enough

some people have scars the world sees

but most have scars inside that breathe

This is Still Me

I hit the wall and fell to my knees.

Wobbly and weak, I could no longer breathe.

I no longer knew this body that turned against me.

My heart became slow and my blood ran thinner,

yet the clock ticked like

movies to a time I remembered,

but this is still me.

My mind slipped and my eyes dimmed,

but my soul cried to let you all in,

because deep inside, this is still me.

Memories clung to the mind I had left

through my repetitive stance,

and you grew weary of listening

to the same old stories I knew,

but I remembered a life I once had with you.

This is a life of uncertainty.

Like my wrinkled elbows to my knees,

this is still me,

so, as I go, let me have my memories

and rest in peace.

Human of Sorrow

Blind eyes don't see pain

or the sorrow of tomorrow

They see worldly gains

and things they can take

But a heart of compassion

breathes the world's pain

like no other, and sees

the gains of lifting others,

because their eyes are upon

the hope of a better world,

even through all the sorrow

The Toll

Just give me a book

and let me dream and stare

Give me the peace and quiet

of a pretty hope somewhere

to warm my cold hands

and encourage my heart

Society demands our time

but our hearts and bodies

scream about the tolls

that take our lives

Reflection

The body decays and slows

it shrinks and stops to grow

Then it rots in the ground

or an urn

and all that is left

are memories, pictures or videos

There comes a time when we must reflect

We must come to terms

with the time we have left

Maybe the end is not near

Perhaps you have many years

If we don't stop through the madness

to reflect why we are here,

then our lives are nothing more

than the hole we rot in

or the shiny urn of the

reflection of those who remain

to grieve and mourn

The Weak Ones

We are vile and weak,

inconsequential and asleep,

unless we can be molded

into something controlled and kept.

We are a burden unless we hold our weight,

or perform under judgments eyes.

Reality shows we will always be swept aside,

no matter how hard we work,

even through the sacrifice.

Are we truly weak, though?

To be the soul of the world

that gives a hope and future

to continue building a world upon.

We are judged to be weak,

but the soul of us

screams we are strong,

because it's the weak ones

who continue holding us back,

we who work to create our own songs.

Even the biggest dams

cannot stop the flood gates,

because what is held back

eventually comes for us all.

Wake

I stood among the rolling clouds,

my eyes withered with self-doubt.

The years of trauma had drove me down

and my knees were cracked and bleeding out.

No one could see my heart of tragedy,

or what it had done to me.

They could not tell the pain had taken me

to the dark places of unending grief.

Until one day, I was ready to stay down,

and die in my pain and drown my sorrows out.

But a lonely soul met me there

and pulled me up from the ground.

Their shoulders were not as

frail as mine or slumped in defeat,

but scars riddled their knees.

As I beheld them with awe and wonder,

they whispered, *I understand what you've been held under,*

and as they reached for the highest cloud,

thunder rolled out like a wake and clapped my weak knees.

Instead of falling back down,

the ground vibrated to keep me on my feet.

The sky screamed as lightening

sprayed over my head

like a crown of veins bleeding out.

The fire cracked the sky open like claws of unrest,

and I turned to them with my eyes burst wide open

as if this were a malicious test.

Their lips spread wide like compassion bled through their life, and this mercy they exuded I had not seen in a long while.

Now, you try, they said,

and then pushed me forward into the sky.

So, I swallowed my doubt and reached out a shaky hand.

After all, they were still alive

from all the times they had bled.

As the lightening touched my fingers and pulled me inside,

I saw a reprieve from the trauma I had been,

and my heart thumped back to life

and my lungs filled with breath again.

We never know who has been subjected

to traumas we could never believe,

but I know that it took a person

who had also been hurt with great pain

with no relief in sight,

to stand beside me and encourage me

to reach for the clouds I never could see,

even through my pain and tragedy.

And now I can stand beside you

and push you, too,

into the clouds where the thunder calls and

the lightening knows your pain,

so, you can breathe anew.

So, off you go

where hope will find you,

but I will stand here beside you,

encouraging you,

until you do.

Pull Me Up Alongside You

When the storms came,

I thought I would drown,

but you pulled me up alongside you

and together, we faced the clouds

You pulled me up alongside you

when my knees gave out,

even at times my lungs

were too weary to shout

When silence prevailed

through rain and doubts,

you pulled me up alongside you

and together, we survived the hardships out

Please Sit Next to Me

I walked along a lonely park road,

the weight of my burdens taking their tolls.

My face stared long and hard into puddles

as the rain trickled down

from this sudden, rainy storm.

An old man met my stare with precision,

and called for me to sit down

under a canopy of protection.

His shoulders slumped with age,

and his body was frail in his last season.

He had no hair under his dark cap,

but it distinguished gray eyes of reason.

Something inside him drew me to the side,

so, I sat on the bench

and looked him in the eyes,

as we waited for the rain to subside.

He sighed deeply, and with great surprise,

told me his story that left tears in my eyes.

And suddenly,

all the mistakes I've ever made

hit me like a freight train.

I opened my mouth, but nothing came out,

as he made me see what life is really about.

He said,

the mistakes I've made have worn me thin,

but grace is given to those who don't give in.

Life throttled pain upon me

sometimes too great to bear,

and if it weren't for hope

that came from somewhere,

I would have died in despair.

He said, thank you for sitting

next to me and hearing me out.

And so, as I did, he turned to finally go,

and the rain swallowed him up,

and the clouds breathed him a new soul.

I sat there perplexed and empowered

with the grace he had shown.

So, I turned to the horizon

as the sun burst out,

and my heart was relieved,

because he also listened to me grieve.

The truth of this encounter hit me suddenly.

One day,

it'll be my turn for the life story to flow,

and I will ask someone

who is also walking a lonely road

to sit next to me through a storm,

because I spent a lifetime learning which way to go.

III:
AMPLIFY

Held Accountable

It rides us hard our whole life,

and society taught us to take it

as it executes malicious pride.

And while it pillages,

it must have thought,

that all of us had been bought.

And many were blind, but many were not,

so, the ones who could see stood.

And while it enjoyed its endless greed

through our captivity,

we crept out to meet the rising dawn.

As the light burst through the darkness

it had manifested with despair,

it held accountable those who refused

to let the captives live and breathe.

As we set them free,

we turned back to face the endless greed,

shouting:

This isn't for you, this is for me,

finally!

Amplify

We're listening to the wrong voices

warning us to be silent over it all,

but injustice isn't partial and doesn't care

as it amplifies the worst of it all.

It screams as it breaks things,

and then hollows out the world's heart.

To amplify the victims is to set free

all of the things that are wrong,

and then turn around and fight for those

who had no voice, at all.

We cannot stop until we amplify them all.

Opportunity

I couldn't go to a job interview,

because I had a toddler in my lap,

and no one to watch him,

and no money for daycare.

I was broken beyond all despair,

and the hiring manager would not allow

a child in the office during a short interview.

So, as I remembered that time in my life,

my employee and I gazed down the hall

at the single mother with the toddler in her lap.

She had dark rings under her eyes,

and as the child squirmed and cried,

I said, bring her in for this interview.

Let's give the child a cookie, and a book or two.

Let's show her we care about her future, too.

And I hired her,

because she already met the qualifications

of the job I posted and needed to do.

Bleed

Fine.

You proved your strength,

and desperate precision.

You proved boundaries are nothing

compared to your ambitions.

So, you made me bleed.

And bleed I will.

But you failed to see

that you'll bleed, too.

Because whether we live or die,

we all bleed the same, we do.

Diamond

It lingers behind walls of earth and doubt

until the right tools dig it out

It's drug to the surface to face the light

and some are unwanted and cast out

But oh, my dear, did you not know?

Jagged rocks can be softened under what's hidden

and priceless treasures offer great ambition

You think you cannot be pulled from your plight,

but you are a diamond meant to shine in the light

The Resolve of Me

I stand on a lonely reprieve

with shaky, weak knees

I race through meadows of grief

hunting to take everything from me

I plummet into chasms of pain

haunting my dreams

I fold into a death roll

as the ground bends to me

This is not the end of me or my dreams

because the sky is higher than me

My knees may reach the ground

but my wings burst out

screaming the resolve of ME

so then,

I can touch the clouds

We Are Not the Same

Is blood really thicker than water?

Does it grow like a tree?

Does it spread its roots

for the whole world to see?

Or is it fearful of change,

and the bubble it breeds?

Does it bend but not break,

and let each person breathe?

Does it stifle hopes

or encourage dreams?

Does it stand tall and fight back,

when darkness comes to play?

Or does it cower to power,

no matter what they say.

Does it build knowledge,

to stand the test of time?

Or does it bury truths,

at the expense of those it has traumatized?

Blood is not thicker than water,

because my people are the ones

who love me for me.

They encourage my growth,

my hopes, and dreams.

They stand and fight for me

when I am weak on my knees,

and do not cower to power,

no matter how they bleed.

I See the Bloom Now

It was far away and I could not reach it

I could only think and hope

to one day feel it

And every time I wanted to shout

I swallowed it back down

and shut my mouth

But the seed planted

would not dry out

We think times are hopeless

until a bloom sprouts up

when everything seems lost

It has a reason to grow

and even through despair,

we see the bloom

The Beauty of You

You are beauty, you are fine

You are strong and graceful,

even if you can never climb

If you don't know or aren't sure enough,

let me encourage you

to stop listening to all the stuff

and ignore the endless fables

The world has no right tell you what you are

So, hold your chin high, and take a deep breath

one day, you will look back

and smile at all these tests

Crave

A sliver of a blade of grass

may mean nothing at all

to the small minded,

or those who care not for

how the world may fall,

but when you see the sliver

among emerald fields of peace,

our eyes should crave to see

more of something so small

that makes this world

a turning masterpiece

Hollow

We enjoy the beauty of a flower,

or the tune of a song.

And even as clouds roar over us

in spite to bring summer along,

the greedy have hollow eyes,

and do not see the differences

through each raging storm.

They take the flowers, tossing them along,

siphoning the air from their lungs,

as they pluck them up, one by one.

They sing their own devious songs,

and it matters not whether it's

a winter or a summer storm,

for the hollow man takes what he sees

through clawed grasps of wrong.

But these are the world's grasp of hope,

that lives and breathes.

You can call them little

young adults until you scream.

You can call them

women or men, sight unseen.

But they are children, who live and breathe.

They are children the hollow will never see.

So, because of their endless greed,

it is up to you and me

to continue to set them free.

The Rock we Knew

It started small, pushing through the floorboards.

Dust danced, floundering in the light streams.

The floor splintered and broke in pieces,

so, we opened the windows and put on some shoes.

The rock we thought was just an old root

took hold of the house and ripped it anew.

The house collapsed and broke into the ravine.

We had been taken, and would've seen it coming,

but we were too busy playing in the dust

floating in the light of the rock we thought we knew.

The Cycle of Hypocrisy

The moon rises and falls,

and daylight comes with the rising dawn.

Fish chase the tides to spawn,

and bears eat the remains so they

can survive the winter storms.

And in the spring,

when snow still kisses the earth,

deer bring their fawns they birthed,

and the forest breathes this cycle of life.

The world marvels in this grace,

encouraging its majesty,

while harnessing its power

to control and take,

because hypocrisy

doesn't care about the rising dawn

or the birthed fawns.

It just cares about what they take

to control it all.

Waterways

Sometimes people only see

the dried-up places

that the world can be

without raising their gaze

to the waterways

that nourish the ground again

when the rain comes down

Different

I prefer colored patches

over the boring stuff that matches

There is no bow in the sky

that's all the same color

The flowers of the rolling fields

may be the same type of flower

but they all have different hues

and shapes and flaws that make them

stand above and still beautiful, after all

Our differences make the world

the beauty it is all about

Our differences make each one of us stand out

The Death Crawl

So, you wanna take me over

and roll like thunder?

So, you wanna scream to the world

that there is no other?

You're blind and fail to see

thunder is nothing compared to lightening

And no one can hear you scream

because the storm has come

to take your dreams

just like you did to people like me

because the truth is, you have no teeth

My Name is a Man

I wrote a horrific story,

but all it did was bring me glory.

They wanted me to show my face

to match the name to the lines I wrote.

So, I met them at their throne,

and stepped into the light they always knew.

And they gawked at me as if they

had been sidelined by a brilliant joke or two.

Because the face behind

the person they thought was a man,

who wrote the story they loved,

was a woman who faced the demand

when the world cried, and said:

we need hope during these painful times!

And it's pathetic I had to hide this light.

Just Take It

I took one for the team

and it cost me my life

Because the air we breathed

had been sown with strife

The water we drank

had been poisoned with greed,

and the food we had eaten

had slowly taken our lives

But we took one for the team

because we were told

this was the way to be

And now, we are deceased,

and people left behind

who are struggling to breathe

must stand and fight

for people like me

Repercussion

It hurts to speak out

because so many do not like the voice

It hurts to step up

because so many are afraid of our choice

and what it means

It hurts to stand

because so many are already on their knees

It hurts to see

because so many are blinded by hurtful things

Oppression fears the repercussions

of people speaking out,

stepping up, and standing for what is right

The consequences of oppression

keeps people weary with need,

but the hope of reverberation

resonates like a demanding echo

And echoes are eventually seen

The Men of my Bones

You were once young and now are grown,

and my heart is full of a hope for your lives

with the knowledge you have learned.

But it is also heavy with grief

as we watch this world burn.

So, no matter what hardships come,

I want you to work hard and laugh, and learn, still.

There are things I hope you always keep,

and one is to protect those who are weak.

Whether it be children, women, animals, or anything.

To always stand for what is right,

to never bend the knee to the greedy,

and do not let the world make you cold and uptight.

To know it's okay to cry at the worlds pain,

to get angry at things that aren't right,

and ponder on things that touch your heart.

Because you may be men,

but you are still human, after all,

no matter what the world has taught.

I hope you never believe in prideful facades,

and that you let values lead you like a flowing spring.

You can be angry at sin,

and all the wrong in the world,

but when you look at this hell on earth,

say, *let me still learn,*

because I want to fix it, not watch it burn.

And to be men of mighty conviction

so other men can look up to you,

and say, I want that for me, too.

And for women to know they can be safe with you,

and never fear for their lives,

because you respect them, too,

because you are men of intention,

who always seek truth and follow it through.

To never cower when others try to entice you,

because you have your own mind and will,

and do not need the crowd to push you.

Be men who have hope and exude mercy,

and that money is not your god, or your life,

but you have the knowledge to build it

so, you can live your life.

Protect and love your spouse

as if they are the very breath of your soul,

and your family you bring into this world.

Stay away from strife, because it will drain your life,

as an equal makes a better partner for your life.

Above all, that you, as men,

always do what is right.

Because men who don't,

always cause the world to fall,

but you can rise above them all.

You need to know, that, as your mother,

I am proud of you all.

I encourage you to carry on,

and lift all men to be courageous and strong,

because that's what it takes

to keep this world moving in the right direction,

all along.

Catalyst

I gazed up from a dark pit as the light shone in,

and warmth spread across my cold, dead skin.

My eyes were blinded by the prison I stayed in,

so, I blinked and blinked until the light sunk in.

It was then I saw the brutal torture of my life,

and the choices I made that put me in this vice.

And as my skin crawled with warmth and light,

I chose to climb out of the pit to end my plight.

And what I once thought was an annoying light,

became the catalyst to finally start living my life.

Vessel

If you are going to pillage the best of me

If you are going to siphon my energy

and treat me like a wobbly branch

that is hacked apart for fun

Then let me be the vessel

for the world to breathe

Let me be the vessel

so the blind can see

and if you must toss me into

a pit of flames

then let the world say

the fire came from me

The Way It Is

It's not okay to say

it is the way it is

when people are oppressed

by the hands of greed,

when people do not have what they need

and the world cannot breathe,

because money matters more than life,

and power matters more than doing what is right

People have a right to live their life,

and the oppressors do not see the human inside

Oppressors do not see the hope of what is right

Instead, they glorify their endless night,

because they are dark inside

People justify the way it is

until someone stands

who is riddled with scars

and pain from self-doubt,

from battles they faced

who nearly did not make it out,

and screams to the world:

No, it is not!

And that's when the light comes in,

because then, the world sees

that the way it is

is *not* the way it should be

or should have ever been